50 Premium Island Bread Recipes for Home

By: Kelly Johnson

Table of Contents

- Hawaiian Sweet Bread
- Jamaican Festival Bread
- Bahamian Coconut Bread
- Barbados Rum Bread
- Puerto Rican Pan Sobao
- Trinidadian Bake
- Cuban Medianoche Bread
- Guadeloupean Pain de Mie
- St. Lucian Cassava Bread
- Grenadian Spice Bread
- Barbadian Bakes
- Virgin Island Johnny Cake
- Bermudian Raisin Bread
- Dominican Arepa Bread
- Anguillian Bread Pudding
- Caymanian Cayman Bread
- Saint Vincent Bread Rolls
- Turks and Caicos Coconut Buns
- Montserrat Cornmeal Bread
- Martinican Pain au Chocolat
- Aruba Pan de Cuca
- Curacao Krentenbrood
- Bonairean Bonchi Bread
- Saint Barthelemy Banana Bread
- Saint Martin Spiced Bread
- Saint Thomas Bread Pudding
- Nevisian Cassava Cake
- Sint Eustatius Bread
- Sint Maarten Sweet Bread
- Tortola Tropical Bread
- Anguilla Rum Cake Bread
- St. Kitts Nutmeg Bread

- Barbuda Spiced Fruit Bread
- Bonairean Maishi Bread
- Saint Eustatius Raisin Loaf
- Saint Barts Pain d'Épices
- Aruba Pan Yaya
- Saint Martin Pineapple Bread
- Guadeloupean Pain d'Ananas
- St. Croix Sugar Bread
- Saint Lucia Banana Nut Bread
- Dominica Coconut Raisin Bread
- British Virgin Islands Cornbread
- Martinique Coconut Loaf
- Curacao Pan Pita
- Tortola Fruitcake Bread
- Saint Barthelemy Coconut Bread
- Nevisian Ginger Bread
- Anguilla Pineapple Bread
- Saint Thomas Sweet Loaf

Hawaiian Sweet Bread

Ingredients:

- 1 cup warm milk
- 1/2 cup sugar
- 1/2 cup melted butter
- 1/2 cup pineapple juice
- 2 teaspoons active dry yeast
- 4 cups all-purpose flour
- 1/2 teaspoon salt
- 2 large eggs

Instructions:

1. Dissolve yeast in warm milk with a tablespoon of sugar. Let sit for 5 minutes until frothy.
2. In a large bowl, mix remaining sugar, melted butter, pineapple juice, and eggs. Add yeast mixture.
3. Gradually add flour and salt, mixing until dough forms. Knead for about 10 minutes until smooth.
4. Place dough in a greased bowl, cover, and let rise in a warm place for about 1 hour, or until doubled.
5. Punch down dough, divide into two parts, and shape into loaves. Place in greased pans.
6. Let rise for another 30 minutes. Preheat oven to 350°F (175°C).
7. Bake for 25-30 minutes or until golden brown. Cool before slicing.

Enjoy your Hawaiian Sweet Bread!

Jamaican Festival Bread

Ingredients:

- 3 cups all-purpose flour
- 1/4 cup sugar
- 1 tablespoon baking powder
- 1/2 teaspoon salt
- 1/4 cup butter, softened
- 1 cup milk
- 1 large egg
- 1 teaspoon vanilla extract
- 1 tablespoon honey (optional)

Instructions:

1. Preheat your oven to 375°F (190°C). Grease a loaf pan.
2. In a large bowl, combine flour, sugar, baking powder, and salt.
3. Cut in the butter until the mixture resembles coarse crumbs.
4. In a separate bowl, whisk together milk, egg, and vanilla extract.
5. Gradually add the wet ingredients to the dry ingredients, mixing until just combined.
6. If using honey, drizzle it into the batter and fold in gently.
7. Pour the batter into the prepared loaf pan.
8. Bake for 30-35 minutes or until a toothpick inserted in the center comes out clean.
9. Let cool in the pan for 10 minutes, then transfer to a wire rack to cool completely.

Enjoy your delicious Jamaican Festival Bread!

Bahamian Coconut Bread

Ingredients:

- 2 cups all-purpose flour
- 1 cup shredded coconut (sweetened or unsweetened, as preferred)
- 1/2 cup sugar
- 1 tablespoon baking powder
- 1/2 teaspoon salt
- 1/2 cup butter, softened
- 1 cup milk
- 1 large egg
- 1 teaspoon vanilla extract

Instructions:

1. Preheat your oven to 350°F (175°C). Grease a loaf pan or line it with parchment paper.
2. In a large bowl, whisk together the flour, sugar, baking powder, and salt.
3. Cut in the softened butter until the mixture resembles coarse crumbs.
4. Stir in the shredded coconut.
5. In a separate bowl, whisk together the milk, egg, and vanilla extract.
6. Gradually add the wet ingredients to the dry ingredients, mixing until just combined.
7. Pour the batter into the prepared loaf pan.
8. Bake for 50-60 minutes, or until a toothpick inserted into the center comes out clean.
9. Let the bread cool in the pan for 10 minutes, then transfer it to a wire rack to cool completely.

Enjoy your Bahamian Coconut Bread!

Barbados Rum Bread

Ingredients:

- 3 cups all-purpose flour
- 1/2 cup sugar
- 1 tablespoon baking powder
- 1/2 teaspoon salt
- 1/2 cup butter, softened
- 1 cup milk
- 1 large egg
- 1/4 cup dark rum
- 1 teaspoon vanilla extract
- 1/2 cup raisins (optional)

Instructions:

1. Preheat your oven to 350°F (175°C). Grease a loaf pan or line it with parchment paper.
2. In a large bowl, mix the flour, sugar, baking powder, and salt.
3. Cut in the butter until the mixture resembles coarse crumbs.
4. In another bowl, whisk together the milk, egg, dark rum, and vanilla extract.
5. Gradually add the wet ingredients to the dry ingredients, mixing until just combined. Fold in raisins if using.
6. Pour the batter into the prepared loaf pan.
7. Bake for 40-45 minutes or until a toothpick inserted in the center comes out clean.
8. Cool in the pan for 10 minutes, then transfer to a wire rack to cool completely.

Enjoy your Barbados Rum Bread!

Puerto Rican Pan Sobao

Ingredients:

- 4 cups all-purpose flour
- 1/2 cup sugar
- 2 teaspoons salt
- 2 tablespoons active dry yeast
- 1 1/2 cups warm water
- 1/4 cup vegetable oil
- 1 large egg

Instructions:

1. Dissolve the yeast in warm water with a pinch of sugar. Let it sit for about 5 minutes until foamy.
2. In a large bowl, combine flour, sugar, and salt.
3. Make a well in the center and add the yeast mixture, oil, and egg.
4. Mix until a dough forms. Knead for about 10 minutes until smooth and elastic.
5. Place the dough in a greased bowl, cover, and let rise in a warm place for 1-2 hours, or until doubled in size.
6. Punch down the dough and shape into a loaf. Place it in a greased loaf pan.
7. Let rise again for about 30 minutes.
8. Preheat oven to 375°F (190°C). Bake for 30-35 minutes or until the bread is golden brown and sounds hollow when tapped.
9. Cool before slicing.

Enjoy your Pan Sobao!

Trinidadian Bake

Ingredients:

- 3 cups all-purpose flour
- 2 teaspoons baking powder
- 1/2 teaspoon salt
- 1/4 cup sugar
- 1/4 cup cold butter
- 1 cup milk (or as needed)
- 1 large egg (optional, for brushing)

Instructions:

1. Preheat your oven to 375°F (190°C). Grease a baking sheet or line it with parchment paper.
2. In a large bowl, sift together the flour, baking powder, salt, and sugar.
3. Cut in the cold butter until the mixture resembles coarse crumbs.
4. Gradually add the milk, stirring until a soft dough forms. You may not need the entire cup of milk—add just enough to bring the dough together.
5. Turn the dough out onto a floured surface and gently knead it a few times until smooth.
6. Roll out the dough to about 1/2 inch thick and cut into rounds or squares using a cookie cutter or knife.
7. Place the cut dough onto the prepared baking sheet.
8. If desired, brush the tops with a beaten egg for a golden finish.
9. Bake for 15-20 minutes, or until the bakes are golden brown and cooked through.
10. Cool on a wire rack before serving.

Enjoy your Trinidadian Bake!

Cuban Medianoche Bread

Ingredients:

- 4 cups all-purpose flour
- 1/4 cup sugar
- 1 tablespoon active dry yeast
- 1 cup warm milk
- 1/2 cup melted butter
- 1/4 cup warm water
- 1 large egg
- 1 teaspoon salt
- 1 tablespoon honey (optional)

Instructions:

1. Dissolve yeast in warm water with a pinch of sugar. Let it sit for about 5 minutes until foamy.
2. In a large bowl, mix flour, sugar, and salt. Make a well in the center.
3. Add yeast mixture, warm milk, melted butter, egg, and honey (if using) to the well. Mix until a dough forms.
4. Knead on a floured surface for about 10 minutes, or until smooth and elastic.
5. Place the dough in a greased bowl, cover, and let it rise in a warm place for 1-2 hours, or until doubled.
6. Punch down the dough and shape it into a loaf. Place it in a greased loaf pan.
7. Let rise for another 30-45 minutes.
8. Preheat oven to 375°F (190°C). Bake for 30-35 minutes, or until the bread is golden and sounds hollow when tapped.
9. Cool before slicing.

Enjoy your Cuban Medianoche Bread!

Guadeloupean Pain de Mie

Ingredients:

- 3 cups all-purpose flour
- 1/4 cup sugar
- 2 teaspoons active dry yeast
- 1 cup warm milk
- 1/4 cup butter, softened
- 1 large egg
- 1 teaspoon salt

Instructions:

1. Preheat your oven to 375°F (190°C) and grease a loaf pan.
2. Dissolve yeast in warm milk with a pinch of sugar. Let it sit for 5-10 minutes until foamy.
3. In a large bowl, mix flour, sugar, and salt. Make a well in the center.
4. Add the yeast mixture, softened butter, and egg to the well. Mix until a dough forms.
5. Knead on a floured surface for about 10 minutes until smooth.
6. Place the dough in a greased bowl, cover with a cloth, and let rise in a warm place for 1-2 hours, or until doubled in size.
7. Punch down the dough, shape it into a loaf, and place it in the prepared pan.
8. Let it rise again for about 30 minutes.
9. Bake for 30-35 minutes, or until golden brown and hollow-sounding when tapped.
10. Cool on a wire rack before slicing.

Enjoy your Pain de Mie from Guadeloupe!

St. Lucian Cassava Bread

Ingredients:

- 3 cups all-purpose flour
- 1/4 cup sugar
- 2 teaspoons active dry yeast
- 1 cup warm milk
- 1/4 cup butter, softened
- 1 large egg
- 1 teaspoon salt

Instructions:

1. Preheat your oven to 375°F (190°C) and grease a loaf pan.
2. Dissolve yeast in warm milk with a pinch of sugar. Let it sit for 5-10 minutes until foamy.
3. In a large bowl, mix flour, sugar, and salt. Make a well in the center.
4. Add the yeast mixture, softened butter, and egg to the well. Mix until a dough forms.
5. Knead on a floured surface for about 10 minutes until smooth.
6. Place the dough in a greased bowl, cover with a cloth, and let rise in a warm place for 1-2 hours, or until doubled in size.
7. Punch down the dough, shape it into a loaf, and place it in the prepared pan.
8. Let it rise again for about 30 minutes.
9. Bake for 30-35 minutes, or until golden brown and hollow-sounding when tapped.
10. Cool on a wire rack before slicing.

Enjoy your Pain de Mie from Guadeloupe!

St. Lucian Cassava Bread

Ingredients:

- 2 cups grated cassava (yucca)
- 1/2 cup grated coconut
- 1/2 cup sugar
- 1 teaspoon baking powder
- 1/2 teaspoon salt
- 1/4 cup melted butter
- 1/2 cup milk (or as needed)
- 1/2 teaspoon ground cinnamon (optional)
- 1/4 teaspoon nutmeg (optional)

Instructions:

1. Preheat your oven to 350°F (175°C) and grease a loaf pan.
2. In a large bowl, mix grated cassava, grated coconut, sugar, baking powder, salt, cinnamon, and nutmeg.
3. Stir in melted butter and enough milk to form a thick batter.
4. Pour the batter into the prepared loaf pan and smooth the top.
5. Bake for 45-50 minutes, or until the bread is firm and golden brown.
6. Cool in the pan for 10 minutes, then transfer to a wire rack to cool completely.

Enjoy your St. Lucian Cassava Bread!

Grenadian Spice Bread

Ingredients:

- 3 cups all-purpose flour
- 1/2 cup sugar
- 2 teaspoons baking powder
- 1 teaspoon ground cinnamon
- 1/2 teaspoon ground nutmeg
- 1/2 teaspoon allspice
- 1/4 teaspoon ground cloves
- 1/2 teaspoon salt
- 1/2 cup butter, softened
- 1 cup milk
- 2 large eggs
- 1/2 cup raisins (optional)
- 1/4 cup dark rum (optional)

Instructions:

1. Preheat your oven to 350°F (175°C) and grease a loaf pan.
2. In a large bowl, combine flour, sugar, baking powder, cinnamon, nutmeg, allspice, cloves, and salt.
3. Cut in the butter until the mixture resembles coarse crumbs.
4. In another bowl, whisk together milk, eggs, and rum (if using).
5. Add the wet ingredients to the dry ingredients and mix until just combined. Fold in raisins if using.
6. Pour the batter into the prepared loaf pan.
7. Bake for 45-50 minutes, or until a toothpick inserted into the center comes out clean.
8. Cool in the pan for 10 minutes, then transfer to a wire rack to cool completely.

Enjoy your Grenadian Spice Bread!

Barbadian Bakes

Ingredients:

- 3 cups all-purpose flour
- 2 teaspoons baking powder
- 1/2 teaspoon salt
- 1/4 cup sugar
- 1/4 cup cold butter
- 1 cup milk (or as needed)
- 1 large egg (optional, for brushing)

Instructions:

1. Preheat your oven to 375°F (190°C) and grease a baking sheet or line it with parchment paper.
2. In a large bowl, sift together flour, baking powder, salt, and sugar.
3. Cut in the cold butter until the mixture resembles coarse crumbs.
4. Gradually add the milk, stirring until a soft dough forms. You may need a bit more or less milk, so add it slowly.
5. Turn the dough out onto a floured surface and gently knead it a few times until smooth.
6. Roll out the dough to about 1/2 inch thick and cut into rounds or squares using a cookie cutter or knife.
7. Place the cut dough onto the prepared baking sheet.
8. If desired, brush the tops with a beaten egg for a golden finish.
9. Bake for 15-20 minutes, or until the bakes are golden brown and cooked through.
10. Cool on a wire rack before serving.

Enjoy your Barbadian Bakes!

Virgin Island Johnny Cake

Ingredients:

- 2 cups all-purpose flour
- 1/4 cup sugar
- 1 tablespoon baking powder
- 1/2 teaspoon salt
- 1/4 cup cold butter
- 3/4 cup milk
- 1 large egg

Instructions:

1. Preheat your oven to 375°F (190°C) and grease a baking pan.
2. In a large bowl, mix flour, sugar, baking powder, and salt.
3. Cut in the cold butter until the mixture resembles coarse crumbs.
4. In another bowl, whisk together milk and egg.
5. Add the wet ingredients to the dry ingredients and stir until just combined.
6. Pour the batter into the prepared pan and smooth the top.
7. Bake for 25-30 minutes, or until the cake is golden brown and a toothpick inserted into the center comes out clean.
8. Cool in the pan for 10 minutes, then transfer to a wire rack to cool completely.

Enjoy your Virgin Island Johnny Cake!

Bermudian Raisin Bread

Ingredients:

- 4 cups all-purpose flour
- 1/2 cup sugar
- 1 tablespoon baking powder
- 1/2 teaspoon salt
- 1/2 cup butter, softened
- 1 cup milk
- 1 large egg
- 1 cup raisins
- 1 teaspoon ground cinnamon (optional)
- 1/4 teaspoon ground nutmeg (optional)

Instructions:

1. Preheat your oven to 350°F (175°C) and grease a loaf pan.
2. In a large bowl, combine flour, sugar, baking powder, salt, cinnamon, and nutmeg.
3. Cut in the butter until the mixture resembles coarse crumbs.
4. Stir in the raisins.
5. In another bowl, whisk together milk and egg.
6. Add the wet ingredients to the dry ingredients and mix until just combined.
7. Pour the batter into the prepared loaf pan.
8. Bake for 50-60 minutes, or until the bread is golden brown and a toothpick inserted into the center comes out clean.
9. Cool in the pan for 10 minutes, then transfer to a wire rack to cool completely.

Enjoy your Bermudian Raisin Bread!

Dominican Arepa Bread

Ingredients:

- 2 cups all-purpose flour
- 1 cup cornmeal
- 1/2 cup sugar
- 1 tablespoon baking powder
- 1/2 teaspoon salt
- 1/2 cup butter, softened
- 1 cup milk
- 2 large eggs
- 1 teaspoon vanilla extract
- 1/2 cup grated cheese (optional, for a savory twist)

Instructions:

1. Preheat your oven to 375°F (190°C) and grease a baking pan or line it with parchment paper.
2. In a large bowl, whisk together the flour, cornmeal, sugar, baking powder, and salt.
3. Cut in the softened butter until the mixture resembles coarse crumbs.
4. In another bowl, whisk together the milk, eggs, and vanilla extract.
5. Gradually add the wet ingredients to the dry ingredients, mixing until just combined.
6. If using cheese, fold it into the batter.
7. Pour the batter into the prepared pan and smooth the top.
8. Bake for 30-35 minutes, or until the bread is golden brown and a toothpick inserted into the center comes out clean.
9. Cool in the pan for 10 minutes, then transfer to a wire rack to cool completely.

Enjoy your Dominican Arepa Bread!

Anguillian Bread Pudding

Ingredients:

- 6 slices of stale bread, torn into pieces
- 2 cups milk
- 1/2 cup sugar
- 1/2 cup raisins (or other dried fruits like currants or sultanas)
- 1/4 cup melted butter
- 3 large eggs
- 1 teaspoon vanilla extract
- 1/2 teaspoon ground cinnamon
- 1/4 teaspoon ground nutmeg
- 1/4 teaspoon salt
- Optional: 1/4 cup dark rum or brandy

Instructions:

1. Preheat your oven to 350°F (175°C) and grease a baking dish.
2. Place the torn bread pieces in a large bowl. Pour the milk over the bread and let it soak for about 10 minutes, or until the bread is fully softened.
3. In another bowl, whisk together the sugar, melted butter, eggs, vanilla extract, cinnamon, nutmeg, and salt.
4. Gently fold the egg mixture into the soaked bread until well combined.
5. Stir in the raisins and rum or brandy, if using.
6. Pour the mixture into the prepared baking dish.
7. Bake for 45-55 minutes, or until the pudding is set and the top is golden brown.
8. Let it cool slightly before serving. Serve warm or at room temperature, optionally with a drizzle of vanilla sauce or a dollop of whipped cream.

Enjoy your Anguillian Bread Pudding!

Caymanian Cayman Bread

Ingredients:

- 3 cups all-purpose flour
- 1/2 cup sugar
- 1 tablespoon baking powder
- 1/2 teaspoon salt
- 1/2 cup butter, softened
- 1 cup milk
- 2 large eggs
- 1/2 cup grated coconut (optional)
- 1/4 cup raisins or dried fruit (optional)
- 1 teaspoon vanilla extract

Instructions:

1. Preheat your oven to 350°F (175°C) and grease a loaf pan or line it with parchment paper.
2. In a large bowl, mix flour, sugar, baking powder, and salt.
3. Cut in the softened butter until the mixture resembles coarse crumbs.
4. In a separate bowl, whisk together milk, eggs, and vanilla extract.
5. Gradually add the wet ingredients to the dry ingredients, mixing until just combined.
6. Fold in grated coconut and raisins or dried fruit if using.
7. Pour the batter into the prepared loaf pan.
8. Bake for 40-45 minutes, or until the bread is golden brown and a toothpick inserted into the center comes out clean.
9. Cool in the pan for 10 minutes, then transfer to a wire rack to cool completely.

Enjoy your Caymanian Cayman Bread!

Saint Vincent Bread Rolls

Ingredients:

- 3 cups all-purpose flour
- 1/2 cup sugar
- 1 tablespoon baking powder
- 1/2 teaspoon salt
- 1/2 cup butter, softened
- 1 cup milk
- 2 large eggs
- 1/2 cup grated coconut (optional)
- 1/4 cup raisins or dried fruit (optional)
- 1 teaspoon vanilla extract

Instructions:

1. Preheat your oven to 350°F (175°C) and grease a loaf pan or line it with parchment paper.
2. In a large bowl, mix flour, sugar, baking powder, and salt.
3. Cut in the softened butter until the mixture resembles coarse crumbs.
4. In a separate bowl, whisk together milk, eggs, and vanilla extract.
5. Gradually add the wet ingredients to the dry ingredients, mixing until just combined.
6. Fold in grated coconut and raisins or dried fruit if using.
7. Pour the batter into the prepared loaf pan.
8. Bake for 40-45 minutes, or until the bread is golden brown and a toothpick inserted into the center comes out clean.
9. Cool in the pan for 10 minutes, then transfer to a wire rack to cool completely.

Enjoy your Caymanian Cayman Bread!

Saint Vincent Bread Rolls

Ingredients:

- 4 cups all-purpose flour
- 1/4 cup sugar
- 2 teaspoons active dry yeast
- 1 1/2 cups warm milk
- 1/4 cup butter, softened
- 1 large egg
- 1 teaspoon salt

Instructions:

1. Dissolve yeast in warm milk with a pinch of sugar. Let it sit for about 5 minutes until foamy.
2. In a large bowl, combine flour, sugar, and salt.
3. Make a well in the center and add the yeast mixture, softened butter, and egg.
4. Mix until a dough forms. Knead on a floured surface for about 10 minutes until smooth and elastic.
5. Place the dough in a greased bowl, cover, and let it rise in a warm place for 1-2 hours, or until doubled.
6. Punch down the dough and divide it into 12-15 equal portions. Shape each portion into a roll and place them on a greased baking sheet.
7. Let the rolls rise again for about 30 minutes.
8. Preheat oven to 375°F (190°C). Bake for 15-20 minutes, or until golden brown.
9. Cool on a wire rack before serving.

Enjoy your Saint Vincent Bread Rolls!

Turks and Caicos Coconut Buns

Ingredients:

- 3 cups all-purpose flour
- 1/2 cup sugar
- 2 teaspoons baking powder
- 1/2 teaspoon salt
- 1/2 cup cold butter, cubed
- 1 cup shredded coconut (sweetened or unsweetened)
- 1 large egg
- 1/2 cup milk
- 1 teaspoon vanilla extract

Instructions:

1. Preheat your oven to 375°F (190°C) and grease a baking sheet or line it with parchment paper.
2. In a large bowl, mix flour, sugar, baking powder, and salt.
3. Cut in the cold butter until the mixture resembles coarse crumbs.
4. Stir in shredded coconut.
5. In a separate bowl, whisk together egg, milk, and vanilla extract.
6. Gradually add the wet ingredients to the dry ingredients, mixing until a dough forms.
7. Drop spoonfuls of dough onto the prepared baking sheet, spacing them about 2 inches apart.
8. Bake for 15-20 minutes, or until the buns are golden brown.
9. Cool on a wire rack before serving.

Enjoy your Turks and Caicos Coconut Buns!

Montserrat Cornmeal Bread

Ingredients:

- 1 cup cornmeal
- 1 cup all-purpose flour
- 1/2 cup sugar
- 2 teaspoons baking powder
- 1/2 teaspoon salt
- 1/2 cup butter, melted
- 1 cup milk
- 2 large eggs
- 1/2 cup grated cheese (optional, for a savory touch)
- 1/2 cup raisins or dried fruit (optional)

Instructions:

1. Preheat your oven to 350°F (175°C) and grease a loaf pan.
2. In a large bowl, combine cornmeal, flour, sugar, baking powder, and salt.
3. In another bowl, whisk together melted butter, milk, and eggs.
4. Gradually add the wet ingredients to the dry ingredients, mixing until just combined. Fold in cheese and/or raisins if using.
5. Pour the batter into the prepared loaf pan.
6. Bake for 40-50 minutes, or until the bread is golden brown and a toothpick inserted into the center comes out clean.
7. Cool in the pan for 10 minutes, then transfer to a wire rack to cool completely.

Enjoy your Montserrat Cornmeal Bread!

Martinican Pain au Chocolat

Ingredients:

For the Dough:

- 3 1/2 cups all-purpose flour
- 1/4 cup sugar
- 1 tablespoon active dry yeast
- 1 cup milk, warmed
- 1/2 cup unsalted butter, softened
- 1 large egg
- 1/2 teaspoon salt

For the Filling:

- 4 ounces dark chocolate bars or chocolate chips

For the Egg Wash:

- 1 large egg, beaten
- 1 tablespoon milk

Instructions:

1. **Prepare the Dough:**
    1. In a small bowl, dissolve the yeast in the warm milk with a pinch of sugar. Let it sit for about 5 minutes until foamy.
    2. In a large bowl, combine flour, sugar, and salt. Make a well in the center.
    3. Add the yeast mixture, softened butter, and egg to the well. Mix until a dough forms.
    4. Knead on a floured surface for about 10 minutes, or until smooth and elastic.
    5. Place the dough in a greased bowl, cover with a cloth, and let it rise in a warm place for about 1-2 hours, or until doubled in size.
2. **Shape the Pain au Chocolat:**
    1. Punch down the dough and turn it out onto a floured surface. Roll it out into a rectangle, about 1/4 inch thick.
    2. Cut the dough into rectangles, each about 4 inches by 6 inches.
    3. Place a piece of chocolate (or a few chocolate chips) in the center of each rectangle.
    4. Fold the dough over the chocolate to form a rectangle, pinching the edges to seal.
3. **Proof and Bake:**

1. Place the shaped pastries on a baking sheet lined with parchment paper. Cover with a cloth and let them rise for about 30 minutes.
2. Preheat your oven to 375°F (190°C).
3. Brush the tops of the pastries with the beaten egg mixed with milk for a shiny finish.
4. Bake for 15-20 minutes, or until golden brown.

4. **Cool and Serve:**
    1. Allow the Pain au Chocolat to cool slightly before serving.

Enjoy your Martinican Pain au Chocolat!

Aruba Pan de Cuca

Ingredients:

- 3 cups all-purpose flour
- 1 cup sugar
- 1 tablespoon baking powder
- 1/2 teaspoon salt
- 1/2 cup butter, softened
- 1 cup milk
- 2 large eggs
- 1 teaspoon vanilla extract
- 1/2 cup grated coconut (optional)
- 1/4 cup raisins or chopped nuts (optional)

Instructions:

1. **Preheat Oven:**
   - Preheat your oven to 350°F (175°C) and grease a loaf pan or line it with parchment paper.
2. **Mix Dry Ingredients:**
   - In a large bowl, whisk together flour, sugar, baking powder, and salt.
3. **Cut in Butter:**
   - Cut in the softened butter until the mixture resembles coarse crumbs.
4. **Combine Wet Ingredients:**
   - In a separate bowl, whisk together milk, eggs, and vanilla extract.
5. **Mix and Add Optional Ingredients:**
   - Gradually add the wet ingredients to the dry ingredients, mixing until just combined. Fold in grated coconut and raisins or nuts if using.
6. **Bake:**
   - Pour the batter into the prepared loaf pan.
   - Bake for 40-45 minutes, or until a toothpick inserted into the center comes out clean and the bread is golden brown.
7. **Cool:**
   - Allow the Pan de Cuca to cool in the pan for 10 minutes, then transfer to a wire rack to cool completely before slicing.

Enjoy your Aruba Pan de Cuca!

Curacao Krentenbrood

Ingredients:

- 3 1/2 cups all-purpose flour
- 1/2 cup sugar
- 1 tablespoon active dry yeast
- 1/2 teaspoon salt
- 1/2 teaspoon ground cinnamon (optional)
- 1/2 teaspoon ground nutmeg (optional)
- 1/2 cup butter, softened
- 1 cup milk, warmed
- 2 large eggs
- 1 cup raisins or currants
- 1/4 cup chopped nuts (optional)

Instructions:

1. **Prepare the Dough:**
    1. Dissolve the yeast in the warmed milk with a pinch of sugar. Let it sit for about 5 minutes until foamy.
    2. In a large bowl, mix flour, sugar, salt, cinnamon, and nutmeg.
    3. Cut in the butter until the mixture resembles coarse crumbs.
    4. Add the yeast mixture, eggs, and mix until a dough forms.
2. **Knead and Rise:**
    1. Turn the dough onto a floured surface and knead for about 10 minutes until smooth and elastic.
    2. Place the dough in a greased bowl, cover, and let it rise in a warm place for 1-2 hours, or until doubled in size.
3. **Shape and Add Fillings:**
    1. Punch down the dough and turn it out onto a floured surface.
    2. Roll it out into a rectangle, then sprinkle raisins or currants and nuts (if using) evenly over the dough.
    3. Roll the dough up tightly and place it in a greased loaf pan.
4. **Final Rise and Bake:**
    1. Cover the pan and let the dough rise again for about 30 minutes.
    2. Preheat your oven to 375°F (190°C).
    3. Bake for 30-35 minutes, or until the bread is golden brown and sounds hollow when tapped.
5. **Cool:**
    1. Let the Krentenbrood cool in the pan for 10 minutes before transferring to a wire rack to cool completely.

Enjoy your Curacao Krentenbrood!

Bonairean Bonchi Bread

Ingredients:

- 2 cups all-purpose flour
- 1/2 cup cornmeal
- 1/2 cup sugar
- 2 teaspoons baking powder
- 1/2 teaspoon salt
- 1/4 cup cold butter, cubed
- 1 cup milk
- 1 large egg
- 1 cup cooked black-eyed peas (bonchi), drained and mashed or lightly mashed
- 1/4 cup chopped fresh parsley (optional for added flavor)

Instructions:

1. **Prepare Oven:**
    - Preheat your oven to 350°F (175°C) and grease a loaf pan or line it with parchment paper.
2. **Mix Dry Ingredients:**
    - In a large bowl, whisk together flour, cornmeal, sugar, baking powder, and salt.
3. **Cut in Butter:**
    - Cut in the cold butter until the mixture resembles coarse crumbs.
4. **Combine Wet Ingredients:**
    - In another bowl, whisk together milk and egg.
5. **Combine Ingredients:**
    - Add the wet ingredients to the dry ingredients and mix until just combined.
    - Fold in the mashed black-eyed peas and parsley if using.
6. **Bake:**
    - Pour the batter into the prepared loaf pan.
    - Bake for 45-50 minutes, or until the bread is golden brown and a toothpick inserted into the center comes out clean.
7. **Cool:**
    - Allow the Bonchi Bread to cool in the pan for 10 minutes, then transfer to a wire rack to cool completely.

Enjoy your Bonairean Bonchi Bread!

Saint Barthelemy Banana Bread

Ingredients:

- 1 1/2 cups all-purpose flour
- 1/2 teaspoon baking soda
- 1/2 teaspoon baking powder
- 1/4 teaspoon salt
- 1/2 teaspoon ground cinnamon (optional)
- 1/2 cup sugar
- 1/4 cup butter, softened
- 2 large eggs
- 1 cup mashed ripe bananas (about 3 medium bananas)
- 1 teaspoon vanilla extract
- 1/4 cup chopped walnuts or pecans (optional)

Instructions:

1. **Preheat Oven:**
   - Preheat your oven to 350°F (175°C) and grease a loaf pan or line it with parchment paper.
2. **Mix Dry Ingredients:**
   - In a bowl, whisk together flour, baking soda, baking powder, salt, and cinnamon (if using).
3. **Cream Butter and Sugar:**
   - In a separate bowl, cream together the sugar and softened butter until light and fluffy.
4. **Add Eggs and Bananas:**
   - Beat in the eggs one at a time, then stir in the mashed bananas and vanilla extract.
5. **Combine Ingredients:**
   - Gradually add the dry ingredients to the wet ingredients, mixing until just combined. Fold in the nuts if using.
6. **Bake:**
   - Pour the batter into the prepared loaf pan and smooth the top.
   - Bake for 55-65 minutes, or until a toothpick inserted into the center comes out clean and the bread is golden brown.
7. **Cool:**
   - Allow the banana bread to cool in the pan for 10 minutes before transferring it to a wire rack to cool completely.

Enjoy your Saint Barthelemy Banana Bread!

Saint Martin Spiced Bread

Ingredients:

- 3 cups all-purpose flour
- 1/2 cup sugar
- 1 tablespoon baking powder
- 1/2 teaspoon salt
- 1 teaspoon ground cinnamon
- 1/2 teaspoon ground nutmeg
- 1/2 teaspoon ground allspice
- 1/4 teaspoon ground cloves
- 1/2 cup unsalted butter, softened
- 1 cup milk
- 2 large eggs
- 1/2 cup raisins or currants (optional)
- 1/2 cup chopped nuts (optional)
- 1 teaspoon vanilla extract

Instructions:

1. **Preheat Oven:**
   - Preheat your oven to 350°F (175°C) and grease a loaf pan or line it with parchment paper.
2. **Mix Dry Ingredients:**
   - In a large bowl, whisk together flour, sugar, baking powder, salt, cinnamon, nutmeg, allspice, and cloves.
3. **Cream Butter and Sugar:**
   - In a separate bowl, cream the softened butter until smooth. Add sugar and continue to cream until light and fluffy.
4. **Combine Wet Ingredients:**
   - Beat in the eggs one at a time, then stir in the milk and vanilla extract.
5. **Combine Ingredients:**
   - Gradually add the dry ingredients to the wet mixture, mixing until just combined.
   - Fold in raisins or currants and nuts if using.
6. **Bake:**
   - Pour the batter into the prepared loaf pan and smooth the top.
   - Bake for 45-55 minutes, or until a toothpick inserted into the center comes out clean and the bread is golden brown.
7. **Cool:**
   - Allow the spiced bread to cool in the pan for 10 minutes before transferring to a wire rack to cool completely.

Enjoy your Saint Martin Spiced Bread!

Saint Thomas Bread Pudding

Ingredients:

- 6 slices of stale bread, torn into pieces
- 2 cups milk
- 1/2 cup sugar
- 1/4 cup butter, melted
- 2 large eggs
- 1 teaspoon vanilla extract
- 1 teaspoon ground cinnamon
- 1/2 teaspoon ground nutmeg
- 1/2 cup raisins or currants
- 1/4 cup chopped nuts (optional)
- 1/4 cup dark rum or brandy (optional)

Instructions:

1. **Preheat Oven:**
    - Preheat your oven to 350°F (175°C) and grease a baking dish.
2. **Prepare Bread:**
    - Place the torn bread pieces in a large bowl. Pour the milk over the bread and let it soak for about 10 minutes, or until the bread is soft and absorbed most of the milk.
3. **Mix Ingredients:**
    - In another bowl, whisk together sugar, melted butter, eggs, vanilla extract, cinnamon, and nutmeg.
    - Stir in the soaked bread mixture, ensuring it's well combined.
    - Fold in raisins, nuts, and rum or brandy if using.
4. **Bake:**
    - Pour the mixture into the prepared baking dish.
    - Bake for 45-55 minutes, or until the pudding is set and the top is golden brown.
5. **Cool and Serve:**
    - Let the bread pudding cool slightly before serving. It can be enjoyed warm or at room temperature, optionally with a drizzle of vanilla sauce or a dollop of whipped cream.

Enjoy your Saint Thomas Bread Pudding!

Nevisian Cassava Cake

Ingredients:

- 2 cups grated cassava (fresh or frozen, thawed and drained)
- 1 cup sugar
- 1/2 cup unsalted butter, melted
- 1/2 cup coconut milk
- 1/4 cup all-purpose flour
- 1/4 teaspoon salt
- 1/2 teaspoon ground cinnamon
- 1/2 teaspoon ground nutmeg
- 1/2 teaspoon vanilla extract
- 1/2 cup raisins or currants (optional)
- 1/4 cup chopped nuts (optional)

Instructions:

1. **Preheat Oven:**
   - Preheat your oven to 350°F (175°C) and grease a baking dish (about 8x8 inches).
2. **Prepare Cassava:**
   - In a large bowl, combine grated cassava with sugar, melted butter, coconut milk, flour, salt, cinnamon, nutmeg, and vanilla extract. Mix well until fully combined.
3. **Add Optional Ingredients:**
   - Fold in raisins or currants and nuts if using.
4. **Bake:**
   - Pour the mixture into the prepared baking dish and smooth the top.
   - Bake for 45-55 minutes, or until the top is golden brown and the cake is set.
5. **Cool:**
   - Allow the cassava cake to cool in the pan for 10 minutes before transferring to a wire rack to cool completely.

Enjoy your Nevisian Cassava Cake!

Sint Eustatius Bread

Ingredients:

- 3 1/2 cups all-purpose flour
- 1/4 cup sugar
- 2 teaspoons active dry yeast
- 1 1/2 teaspoons salt
- 1 cup warm milk (110°F/45°C)
- 1/4 cup unsalted butter, melted
- 2 large eggs
- 1 teaspoon vanilla extract (optional)

Instructions:

1. **Activate Yeast:**
   - In a small bowl, dissolve the yeast in warm milk with a pinch of sugar. Let it sit for about 5 minutes until foamy.
2. **Mix Dry Ingredients:**
   - In a large bowl, combine flour, sugar, and salt.
3. **Combine Wet Ingredients:**
   - In a separate bowl, whisk together melted butter, eggs, and vanilla extract (if using).
4. **Combine Ingredients:**
   - Make a well in the center of the dry ingredients and pour in the yeast mixture and wet ingredients.
   - Mix until a dough forms. Turn out onto a floured surface and knead for about 10 minutes, or until the dough is smooth and elastic.
5. **First Rise:**
   - Place the dough in a greased bowl, cover with a cloth, and let it rise in a warm place for 1-2 hours, or until doubled in size.
6. **Shape and Second Rise:**
   - Punch down the dough and turn it onto a floured surface. Shape into a loaf or divide into smaller rolls.
   - Place the shaped dough into a greased loaf pan or on a baking sheet for rolls. Cover and let rise for another 30-45 minutes.
7. **Bake:**
   - Preheat your oven to 375°F (190°C).
   - Bake the loaf for 30-35 minutes, or until the bread is golden brown and sounds hollow when tapped. If baking rolls, they may take 15-20 minutes.
8. **Cool:**
   - Let the bread cool in the pan for 10 minutes before transferring to a wire rack to cool completely.

Enjoy your Sint Eustatius Bread!

Sint Maarten Sweet Bread

Ingredients:

- 3 1/2 cups all-purpose flour
- 1/2 cup sugar
- 1 tablespoon baking powder
- 1/2 teaspoon salt
- 1/2 cup unsalted butter, softened
- 1 cup milk
- 2 large eggs
- 1 teaspoon vanilla extract
- 1/2 cup raisins or currants (optional)
- 1/2 cup chopped nuts (optional)

Instructions:

1. **Preheat Oven:**
   - Preheat your oven to 350°F (175°C) and grease a loaf pan or line it with parchment paper.
2. **Mix Dry Ingredients:**
   - In a large bowl, whisk together flour, sugar, baking powder, and salt.
3. **Cream Butter and Sugar:**
   - In a separate bowl, cream the softened butter until smooth. Add sugar and continue to cream until light and fluffy.
4. **Combine Wet Ingredients:**
   - Beat in the eggs one at a time, then stir in milk and vanilla extract.
5. **Combine Ingredients:**
   - Gradually add the dry ingredients to the wet mixture, mixing until just combined. Fold in raisins or currants and nuts if using.
6. **Bake:**
   - Pour the batter into the prepared loaf pan and smooth the top.
   - Bake for 45-55 minutes, or until the bread is golden brown and a toothpick inserted into the center comes out clean.
7. **Cool:**
   - Allow the sweet bread to cool in the pan for 10 minutes before transferring to a wire rack to cool completely.

Enjoy your Sint Maarten Sweet Bread!

Tortola Tropical Bread

Ingredients:

- 2 1/2 cups all-purpose flour
- 1/2 cup sugar
- 1 tablespoon baking powder
- 1/2 teaspoon salt
- 1/2 cup unsalted butter, softened
- 1 cup crushed pineapple, drained
- 1/2 cup shredded coconut
- 1/2 cup chopped mango or papaya (optional)
- 1 large egg
- 1 cup milk
- 1 teaspoon vanilla extract

Instructions:

1. **Preheat Oven:**
   - Preheat your oven to 350°F (175°C) and grease a loaf pan or line it with parchment paper.
2. **Mix Dry Ingredients:**
   - In a large bowl, whisk together flour, sugar, baking powder, and salt.
3. **Cream Butter and Sugar:**
   - In another bowl, cream the softened butter until smooth. Add sugar and continue to cream until light and fluffy.
4. **Combine Wet Ingredients:**
   - Beat in the egg, then stir in milk and vanilla extract.
5. **Combine Ingredients:**
   - Gradually add the dry ingredients to the wet mixture, mixing until just combined. Fold in crushed pineapple, shredded coconut, and chopped mango or papaya if using.
6. **Bake:**
   - Pour the batter into the prepared loaf pan and smooth the top.
   - Bake for 50-60 minutes, or until the bread is golden brown and a toothpick inserted into the center comes out clean.
7. **Cool:**
   - Allow the tropical bread to cool in the pan for 10 minutes before transferring to a wire rack to cool completely.

Enjoy your Tortola Tropical Bread!

Anguilla Rum Cake Bread

Ingredients:

- 2 1/2 cups all-purpose flour
- 1 cup sugar
- 1 tablespoon baking powder
- 1/2 teaspoon salt
- 1/2 cup unsalted butter, softened
- 1 cup milk
- 2 large eggs
- 1/2 cup dark rum
- 1/2 cup chopped nuts (optional)
- 1/2 cup raisins or currants
- 1 teaspoon vanilla extract
- 1/2 teaspoon ground cinnamon (optional)
- 1/4 teaspoon ground nutmeg (optional)

For the Rum Glaze:

- 1/4 cup unsalted butter
- 1/4 cup sugar
- 1/4 cup dark rum

Instructions:

1. **Preheat Oven:**
   - Preheat your oven to 350°F (175°C) and grease a loaf pan or line it with parchment paper.
2. **Mix Dry Ingredients:**
   - In a large bowl, whisk together flour, sugar, baking powder, salt, cinnamon, and nutmeg.
3. **Cream Butter and Sugar:**
   - In another bowl, cream the softened butter until smooth. Add sugar and continue to cream until light and fluffy.
4. **Combine Wet Ingredients:**
   - Beat in the eggs one at a time, then stir in milk, rum, and vanilla extract.
5. **Combine Ingredients:**
   - Gradually add the dry ingredients to the wet mixture, mixing until just combined. Fold in chopped nuts and raisins or currants.
6. **Bake:**
   - Pour the batter into the prepared loaf pan and smooth the top.

- Bake for 50-60 minutes, or until the bread is golden brown and a toothpick inserted into the center comes out clean.
7. **Prepare the Glaze:**
    - While the bread is baking, prepare the rum glaze. In a small saucepan, melt the butter over medium heat. Stir in the sugar and cook until the mixture is bubbly. Remove from heat and stir in the rum.
8. **Apply the Glaze:**
    - When the bread is done baking, let it cool in the pan for 10 minutes. While still warm, brush the rum glaze over the top of the bread. Let the bread cool completely on a wire rack.

Enjoy your Anguilla Rum Cake Bread!

St. Kitts Nutmeg Bread

Ingredients:

- 2 1/2 cups all-purpose flour
- 1 cup sugar
- 1 tablespoon baking powder
- 1/2 teaspoon salt
- 1/2 cup unsalted butter, softened
- 1 cup milk
- 2 large eggs
- 1/2 cup dark rum
- 1/2 cup chopped nuts (optional)
- 1/2 cup raisins or currants
- 1 teaspoon vanilla extract
- 1/2 teaspoon ground cinnamon (optional)
- 1/4 teaspoon ground nutmeg (optional)

For the Rum Glaze:

- 1/4 cup unsalted butter
- 1/4 cup sugar
- 1/4 cup dark rum

Instructions:

1. **Preheat Oven:**
   - Preheat your oven to 350°F (175°C) and grease a loaf pan or line it with parchment paper.
2. **Mix Dry Ingredients:**
   - In a large bowl, whisk together flour, sugar, baking powder, salt, cinnamon, and nutmeg.
3. **Cream Butter and Sugar:**
   - In another bowl, cream the softened butter until smooth. Add sugar and continue to cream until light and fluffy.
4. **Combine Wet Ingredients:**
   - Beat in the eggs one at a time, then stir in milk, rum, and vanilla extract.
5. **Combine Ingredients:**
   - Gradually add the dry ingredients to the wet mixture, mixing until just combined. Fold in chopped nuts and raisins or currants.
6. **Bake:**
   - Pour the batter into the prepared loaf pan and smooth the top.

- Bake for 50-60 minutes, or until the bread is golden brown and a toothpick inserted into the center comes out clean.

7. **Prepare the Glaze:**
    - While the bread is baking, prepare the rum glaze. In a small saucepan, melt the butter over medium heat. Stir in the sugar and cook until the mixture is bubbly. Remove from heat and stir in the rum.

8. **Apply the Glaze:**
    - When the bread is done baking, let it cool in the pan for 10 minutes. While still warm, brush the rum glaze over the top of the bread. Let the bread cool completely on a wire rack.

Enjoy your Anguilla Rum Cake Bread!

St. Kitts Nutmeg Bread

Ingredients:

- 3 cups all-purpose flour
- 1/2 cup sugar
- 1 tablespoon baking powder
- 1/2 teaspoon salt
- 1 teaspoon ground nutmeg
- 1/2 teaspoon ground cinnamon (optional)
- 1/2 cup unsalted butter, softened
- 1 cup milk
- 2 large eggs
- 1/2 cup chopped walnuts or pecans (optional)
- 1/2 cup raisins or currants (optional)
- 1 teaspoon vanilla extract

Instructions:

1. **Preheat Oven:**
   - Preheat your oven to 350°F (175°C) and grease a loaf pan or line it with parchment paper.
2. **Mix Dry Ingredients:**
   - In a large bowl, whisk together flour, sugar, baking powder, salt, nutmeg, and cinnamon (if using).
3. **Cream Butter and Sugar:**
   - In a separate bowl, cream the softened butter until smooth. Add sugar and continue to cream until light and fluffy.
4. **Combine Wet Ingredients:**
   - Beat in the eggs one at a time, then stir in milk and vanilla extract.
5. **Combine Ingredients:**
   - Gradually add the dry ingredients to the wet mixture, mixing until just combined. Fold in chopped nuts and raisins or currants if using.
6. **Bake:**
   - Pour the batter into the prepared loaf pan and smooth the top.
   - Bake for 45-55 minutes, or until the bread is golden brown and a toothpick inserted into the center comes out clean.
7. **Cool:**
   - Allow the nutmeg bread to cool in the pan for 10 minutes before transferring to a wire rack to cool completely.

Enjoy your St. Kitts Nutmeg Bread!

Barbuda Spiced Fruit Bread

Ingredients:

- 3 cups all-purpose flour
- 1/2 cup sugar
- 1 tablespoon baking powder
- 1/2 teaspoon salt
- 1 teaspoon ground cinnamon
- 1/2 teaspoon ground nutmeg
- 1/2 teaspoon ground allspice
- 1/4 teaspoon ground cloves
- 1/2 cup unsalted butter, softened
- 1 cup milk
- 2 large eggs
- 1 cup mixed dried fruits (such as raisins, currants, chopped dates, and dried apricots)
- 1/2 cup chopped nuts (optional)
- 1 teaspoon vanilla extract

Instructions:

1. **Preheat Oven:**
    - Preheat your oven to 350°F (175°C) and grease a loaf pan or line it with parchment paper.
2. **Mix Dry Ingredients:**
    - In a large bowl, whisk together flour, sugar, baking powder, salt, cinnamon, nutmeg, allspice, and cloves.
3. **Cream Butter and Sugar:**
    - In a separate bowl, cream the softened butter until smooth. Add sugar and continue to cream until light and fluffy.
4. **Combine Wet Ingredients:**
    - Beat in the eggs one at a time, then stir in milk and vanilla extract.
5. **Combine Ingredients:**
    - Gradually add the dry ingredients to the wet mixture, mixing until just combined. Fold in the mixed dried fruits and nuts if using.
6. **Bake:**
    - Pour the batter into the prepared loaf pan and smooth the top.
    - Bake for 50-60 minutes, or until the bread is golden brown and a toothpick inserted into the center comes out clean.
7. **Cool:**
    - Allow the spiced fruit bread to cool in the pan for 10 minutes before transferring to a wire rack to cool completely.

Enjoy your Barbuda Spiced Fruit Bread!

Barbuda Spiced Fruit Bread

Ingredients:

- 2 1/2 cups all-purpose flour
- 1/2 cup sugar
- 1 tablespoon baking powder
- 1/2 teaspoon salt
- 1 teaspoon ground cinnamon
- 1/2 teaspoon ground nutmeg
- 1/4 teaspoon ground cloves
- 1/2 cup unsalted butter, softened
- 1 cup milk
- 2 large eggs
- 1 cup mixed dried fruits (e.g., raisins, currants, chopped dates)
- 1/2 cup chopped nuts (e.g., walnuts or pecans, optional)
- 1/4 cup orange juice or dark rum (optional for extra flavor)

Instructions:

1. **Preheat Oven:**
    - Preheat your oven to 350°F (175°C). Grease a loaf pan or line it with parchment paper.
2. **Mix Dry Ingredients:**
    - In a large bowl, whisk together flour, sugar, baking powder, salt, cinnamon, nutmeg, and cloves.
3. **Cream Butter and Sugar:**
    - In a separate bowl, cream the softened butter until smooth. Add sugar and continue to cream until light and fluffy.
4. **Combine Wet Ingredients:**
    - Beat in the eggs one at a time, then stir in the milk and orange juice or dark rum if using.
5. **Combine Ingredients:**
    - Gradually add the dry ingredients to the wet mixture, mixing until just combined. Fold in the dried fruits and nuts if using.
6. **Bake:**
    - Pour the batter into the prepared loaf pan and smooth the top.
    - Bake for 50-60 minutes, or until the bread is golden brown and a toothpick inserted into the center comes out clean.
7. **Cool:**
    - Allow the spiced fruit bread to cool in the pan for about 10 minutes before transferring to a wire rack to cool completely.

Enjoy your Barbuda Spiced Fruit Bread!

Bonairean Maishi Bread

Ingredients:

- 2 cups grated cassava (fresh or frozen, thawed and well-drained)
- 1 cup all-purpose flour
- 1/2 cup cornmeal
- 1/2 cup sugar
- 1/2 teaspoon baking powder
- 1/2 teaspoon salt
- 1/2 teaspoon ground cinnamon (optional)
- 1/2 cup unsalted butter, melted
- 1/2 cup milk
- 2 large eggs
- 1 teaspoon vanilla extract
- 1/2 cup raisins or dried fruit (optional)
- 1/4 cup chopped nuts (optional)

Instructions:

1. **Preheat Oven:**
   - Preheat your oven to 350°F (175°C). Grease a loaf pan or line it with parchment paper.
2. **Prepare Cassava:**
   - If using fresh cassava, peel, grate it, and squeeze out excess moisture using a cheesecloth or paper towels. If using frozen cassava, thaw and drain it thoroughly.
3. **Mix Dry Ingredients:**
   - In a large bowl, whisk together flour, cornmeal, sugar, baking powder, salt, and cinnamon (if using).
4. **Combine Wet Ingredients:**
   - In another bowl, mix melted butter, milk, eggs, and vanilla extract.
5. **Combine Ingredients:**
   - Stir the grated cassava into the wet mixture. Gradually add the dry mixture, mixing until well combined. Fold in raisins or dried fruit and nuts if using.
6. **Pour and Smooth:**
   - Pour the batter into the prepared loaf pan and smooth the top.
7. **Bake:**
   - Bake for 50-60 minutes, or until the bread is golden brown and a toothpick inserted into the center comes out clean.
8. **Cool:**
   - Let the Maishi Bread cool in the pan for about 10 minutes before transferring to a wire rack to cool completely.

Enjoy your Bonairean Maishi Bread!

Saint Eustatius Raisin Loaf

Ingredients:

- 3 cups all-purpose flour
- 1/2 cup sugar
- 1 tablespoon baking powder
- 1/2 teaspoon salt
- 1 teaspoon ground cinnamon
- 1/2 teaspoon ground nutmeg
- 1/2 cup unsalted butter, softened
- 1 cup milk
- 2 large eggs
- 1 cup raisins
- 1 teaspoon vanilla extract
- 1/2 cup chopped nuts (optional)

Instructions:

1. **Preheat Oven:**
   - Preheat your oven to 350°F (175°C). Grease a loaf pan or line it with parchment paper.
2. **Mix Dry Ingredients:**
   - In a large bowl, whisk together flour, sugar, baking powder, salt, cinnamon, and nutmeg.
3. **Cream Butter and Sugar:**
   - In another bowl, cream the softened butter until smooth. Add sugar and continue to cream until light and fluffy.
4. **Combine Wet Ingredients:**
   - Beat in the eggs one at a time, then stir in milk and vanilla extract.
5. **Combine Ingredients:**
   - Gradually add the dry ingredients to the wet mixture, mixing until just combined. Fold in raisins and nuts if using.
6. **Pour and Smooth:**
   - Pour the batter into the prepared loaf pan and smooth the top.
7. **Bake:**
   - Bake for 50-60 minutes, or until the loaf is golden brown and a toothpick inserted into the center comes out clean.
8. **Cool:**
   - Let the raisin loaf cool in the pan for about 10 minutes before transferring to a wire rack to cool completely.

Enjoy your Saint Eustatius Raisin Loaf!

Saint Barts Pain d'Épices

Ingredients:

- 1 1/2 cups all-purpose flour
- 1/2 cup rye flour (optional, for a richer flavor)
- 1/2 cup honey
- 1/2 cup brown sugar
- 1/2 cup milk
- 1/2 cup unsalted butter, softened
- 1 large egg
- 1 teaspoon baking soda
- 1 teaspoon ground cinnamon
- 1/2 teaspoon ground cloves
- 1/2 teaspoon ground nutmeg
- 1/2 teaspoon ground ginger
- 1/4 teaspoon ground cardamom (optional)
- 1/4 cup candied orange peel, chopped (optional)
- 1/4 cup chopped nuts or dried fruit (optional)

Instructions:

1. **Preheat Oven:**
   - Preheat your oven to 350°F (175°C). Grease a loaf pan or line it with parchment paper.
2. **Prepare Wet Ingredients:**
   - In a large bowl, combine honey, brown sugar, milk, and softened butter. Mix until the sugar is dissolved and the mixture is smooth.
3. **Mix Dry Ingredients:**
   - In another bowl, whisk together all-purpose flour, rye flour (if using), baking soda, cinnamon, cloves, nutmeg, ginger, and cardamom (if using).
4. **Combine Ingredients:**
   - Beat the egg into the wet mixture. Gradually add the dry ingredients to the wet mixture, stirring until just combined.
5. **Add Extras:**
   - Fold in candied orange peel, nuts, or dried fruit if using.
6. **Pour and Smooth:**
   - Pour the batter into the prepared loaf pan and smooth the top.
7. **Bake:**
   - Bake for 45-55 minutes, or until the bread is golden brown and a toothpick inserted into the center comes out clean.
8. **Cool:**

- Allow the Pain d'Épices to cool in the pan for about 10 minutes, then transfer to a wire rack to cool completely.

This Pain d'Épices is delicious on its own or served with a spread of butter or cheese. Enjoy your Saint Barthélemy-inspired spiced bread!

Aruba Pan Yaya

Ingredients:

- 3 1/2 cups all-purpose flour
- 1/4 cup sugar
- 1 tablespoon active dry yeast
- 1 teaspoon salt
- 1/2 cup unsalted butter, softened
- 1 cup warm milk (110°F/45°C)
- 2 large eggs
- 1 teaspoon vanilla extract
- 1/2 teaspoon ground nutmeg (optional)
- 1/4 cup raisins or currants (optional)

Instructions:

1. **Prepare Yeast Mixture:**
    - In a small bowl, combine the warm milk and sugar. Sprinkle the yeast on top and let it sit for 5-10 minutes, until it becomes frothy.
2. **Mix Dry Ingredients:**
    - In a large bowl, whisk together flour and salt.
3. **Cream Butter:**
    - In a separate bowl, cream the softened butter until smooth.
4. **Combine Wet Ingredients:**
    - Beat in the eggs one at a time into the creamed butter. Add the vanilla extract and mix well.
5. **Combine Ingredients:**
    - Pour the yeast mixture into the wet ingredients and mix until combined. Gradually add the dry ingredients to the wet mixture, stirring until a dough forms.
6. **Knead Dough:**
    - Turn the dough out onto a floured surface and knead for about 8-10 minutes, or until the dough is smooth and elastic. If using raisins or currants, fold them in during the last few minutes of kneading.
7. **First Rise:**
    - Place the dough in a greased bowl, cover it with a cloth, and let it rise in a warm place for 1-2 hours, or until doubled in size.
8. **Shape and Second Rise:**
    - Punch down the dough and shape it into a loaf or divide it into smaller pieces for rolls. Place in a greased loaf pan or on a baking sheet for rolls. Cover and let rise for another 30-45 minutes.
9. **Bake:**

- Preheat your oven to 350°F (175°C). Bake the loaf for 30-35 minutes, or until golden brown and a toothpick inserted into the center comes out clean.
10. **Cool:**
    - Allow the Pan Yaya to cool in the pan for 10 minutes before transferring to a wire rack to cool completely.

Enjoy your Aruba Pan Yaya! This bread is perfect for breakfast or as a snack with a bit of butter.

Saint Martin Pineapple Bread

Ingredients:

- 2 1/2 cups all-purpose flour
- 1/2 cup sugar
- 1 tablespoon baking powder
- 1/2 teaspoon salt
- 1/2 teaspoon ground cinnamon (optional)
- 1/2 cup unsalted butter, softened
- 1 cup crushed pineapple, well-drained
- 1/2 cup milk
- 2 large eggs
- 1 teaspoon vanilla extract
- 1/4 cup chopped walnuts or pecans (optional)

Instructions:

1. **Preheat Oven:**
    - Preheat your oven to 350°F (175°C). Grease a loaf pan or line it with parchment paper.
2. **Mix Dry Ingredients:**
    - In a large bowl, whisk together flour, sugar, baking powder, salt, and cinnamon (if using).
3. **Cream Butter and Sugar:**
    - In a separate bowl, cream the softened butter until smooth. Add sugar and continue to cream until light and fluffy.
4. **Combine Wet Ingredients:**
    - Beat in the eggs one at a time, then stir in milk, crushed pineapple, and vanilla extract.
5. **Combine Ingredients:**
    - Gradually add the dry ingredients to the wet mixture, mixing until just combined. Fold in chopped nuts if using.
6. **Pour and Smooth:**
    - Pour the batter into the prepared loaf pan and smooth the top.
7. **Bake:**
    - Bake for 50-60 minutes, or until the bread is golden brown and a toothpick inserted into the center comes out clean.
8. **Cool:**
    - Let the pineapple bread cool in the pan for about 10 minutes before transferring to a wire rack to cool completely.

Enjoy your Saint Martin Pineapple Bread! It's perfect for a tropical twist on your bread routine.

Guadeloupean Pain d'Ananas

Ingredients:

- 2 1/2 cups all-purpose flour
- 1/2 cup sugar
- 1 tablespoon baking powder
- 1/2 teaspoon salt
- 1/2 teaspoon ground cinnamon (optional)
- 1/2 cup unsalted butter, softened
- 1 cup crushed pineapple, well-drained
- 1/2 cup milk
- 2 large eggs
- 1 teaspoon vanilla extract
- 1/4 cup chopped pecans or walnuts (optional)

Instructions:

1. **Preheat Oven:**
    - Preheat your oven to 350°F (175°C). Grease a loaf pan or line it with parchment paper.
2. **Mix Dry Ingredients:**
    - In a large bowl, whisk together flour, sugar, baking powder, salt, and cinnamon (if using).
3. **Cream Butter and Sugar:**
    - In a separate bowl, cream the softened butter until smooth. Add sugar and continue to cream until light and fluffy.
4. **Combine Wet Ingredients:**
    - Beat in the eggs one at a time, then stir in milk, crushed pineapple, and vanilla extract.
5. **Combine Ingredients:**
    - Gradually add the dry ingredients to the wet mixture, mixing until just combined. Fold in chopped nuts if using.
6. **Pour and Smooth:**
    - Pour the batter into the prepared loaf pan and smooth the top.
7. **Bake:**
    - Bake for 50-60 minutes, or until the bread is golden brown and a toothpick inserted into the center comes out clean.
8. **Cool:**
    - Allow the Pain d'Ananas to cool in the pan for about 10 minutes before transferring to a wire rack to cool completely.

Enjoy your Guadeloupean Pain d'Ananas! This pineapple bread is perfect for a tropical treat or a flavorful breakfast.

St. Croix Sugar Bread

Ingredients:

- 3 cups all-purpose flour
- 1/2 cup sugar
- 1 tablespoon baking powder
- 1/2 teaspoon salt
- 1/2 teaspoon ground cinnamon (optional)
- 1/2 cup unsalted butter, softened
- 1 cup milk
- 2 large eggs
- 1 teaspoon vanilla extract
- 1/4 cup additional sugar for topping
- 1 teaspoon ground cinnamon for topping (optional)

Instructions:

1. **Preheat Oven:**
    - Preheat your oven to 350°F (175°C). Grease a loaf pan or line it with parchment paper.
2. **Mix Dry Ingredients:**
    - In a large bowl, whisk together flour, sugar, baking powder, salt, and cinnamon (if using).
3. **Cream Butter and Sugar:**
    - In a separate bowl, cream the softened butter until smooth. Add sugar and continue to cream until light and fluffy.
4. **Combine Wet Ingredients:**
    - Beat in the eggs one at a time, then stir in milk and vanilla extract.
5. **Combine Ingredients:**
    - Gradually add the dry ingredients to the wet mixture, mixing until just combined.
6. **Pour and Smooth:**
    - Pour the batter into the prepared loaf pan and smooth the top.
7. **Prepare Topping:**
    - In a small bowl, mix the additional sugar with ground cinnamon. Sprinkle this mixture evenly over the top of the batter.
8. **Bake:**
    - Bake for 45-55 minutes, or until the bread is golden brown and a toothpick inserted into the center comes out clean.
9. **Cool:**
    - Allow the sugar bread to cool in the pan for about 10 minutes before transferring to a wire rack to cool completely.

Enjoy your St. Croix Sugar Bread! It's a wonderfully sweet treat that pairs perfectly with coffee or tea.

Saint Lucia Banana Nut Bread

Ingredients:

- 1 1/2 cups all-purpose flour
- 1 cup sugar
- 1 teaspoon baking powder
- 1/2 teaspoon baking soda
- 1/2 teaspoon salt
- 1/2 teaspoon ground cinnamon (optional)
- 1/2 cup unsalted butter, softened
- 2 large eggs
- 1 cup mashed ripe bananas (about 2-3 bananas)
- 1/4 cup milk
- 1 teaspoon vanilla extract
- 1/2 cup chopped walnuts or pecans

Instructions:

1. **Preheat Oven:**
   - Preheat your oven to 350°F (175°C). Grease a loaf pan or line it with parchment paper.
2. **Mix Dry Ingredients:**
   - In a large bowl, whisk together flour, sugar, baking powder, baking soda, salt, and cinnamon (if using).
3. **Cream Butter and Sugar:**
   - In a separate bowl, cream the softened butter until smooth. Add sugar and continue to cream until light and fluffy.
4. **Combine Wet Ingredients:**
   - Beat in the eggs one at a time. Stir in mashed bananas, milk, and vanilla extract.
5. **Combine Ingredients:**
   - Gradually add the dry ingredients to the wet mixture, mixing until just combined. Fold in the chopped nuts.
6. **Pour and Smooth:**
   - Pour the batter into the prepared loaf pan and smooth the top.
7. **Bake:**
   - Bake for 50-60 minutes, or until the bread is golden brown and a toothpick inserted into the center comes out clean.
8. **Cool:**
   - Allow the banana nut bread to cool in the pan for about 10 minutes before transferring to a wire rack to cool completely.

Enjoy your Saint Lucia Banana Nut Bread! It's perfect for breakfast or as a comforting snack.

Dominica Coconut Raisin Bread

Ingredients:

- 2 1/2 cups all-purpose flour
- 1/2 cup sugar
- 1 tablespoon baking powder
- 1/2 teaspoon salt
- 1/2 cup shredded coconut (sweetened or unsweetened)
- 1/2 cup raisins
- 1/2 cup unsalted butter, softened
- 1 cup milk
- 2 large eggs
- 1 teaspoon vanilla extract

Instructions:

1. **Preheat Oven:**
   - Preheat your oven to 350°F (175°C). Grease a loaf pan or line it with parchment paper.
2. **Mix Dry Ingredients:**
   - In a large bowl, whisk together flour, sugar, baking powder, and salt. Stir in shredded coconut and raisins.
3. **Cream Butter and Sugar:**
   - In a separate bowl, cream the softened butter until smooth. Add sugar and continue to cream until light and fluffy.
4. **Combine Wet Ingredients:**
   - Beat in the eggs one at a time, then stir in milk and vanilla extract.
5. **Combine Ingredients:**
   - Gradually add the dry ingredients to the wet mixture, mixing until just combined.
6. **Pour and Smooth:**
   - Pour the batter into the prepared loaf pan and smooth the top.
7. **Bake:**
   - Bake for 50-60 minutes, or until the bread is golden brown and a toothpick inserted into the center comes out clean.
8. **Cool:**
   - Allow the coconut raisin bread to cool in the pan for about 10 minutes before transferring to a wire rack to cool completely.

Enjoy your Dominica Coconut Raisin Bread! It's perfect for a tropical twist on your bread routine.

British Virgin Islands Cornbread

Ingredients:

- 1 cup cornmeal
- 1 cup all-purpose flour
- 1/4 cup sugar
- 1 tablespoon baking powder
- 1/2 teaspoon salt
- 1/2 cup unsalted butter, melted
- 1 cup milk
- 2 large eggs
- 1 cup creamed corn (optional, for extra moisture and flavor)
- 1/2 cup shredded cheddar cheese (optional, for a cheesy version)

Instructions:

1. **Preheat Oven:**
   - Preheat your oven to 400°F (200°C). Grease a baking dish or cast-iron skillet.
2. **Mix Dry Ingredients:**
   - In a large bowl, whisk together cornmeal, flour, sugar, baking powder, and salt.
3. **Combine Wet Ingredients:**
   - In another bowl, whisk together melted butter, milk, and eggs. Stir in the creamed corn if using.
4. **Combine Ingredients:**
   - Pour the wet ingredients into the dry ingredients and stir until just combined. Fold in shredded cheese if using.
5. **Pour and Smooth:**
   - Pour the batter into the prepared baking dish or skillet and smooth the top.
6. **Bake:**
   - Bake for 20-25 minutes, or until the cornbread is golden brown and a toothpick inserted into the center comes out clean.
7. **Cool:**
   - Allow the cornbread to cool slightly before slicing.

Enjoy your British Virgin Islands Cornbread! It's perfect as a side dish or on its own with a bit of butter.

Martinique Coconut Loaf

Ingredients:

- 1 1/2 cups all-purpose flour
- 1 cup shredded coconut (sweetened or unsweetened)
- 1 cup sugar
- 1 tablespoon baking powder
- 1/2 teaspoon salt
- 1/2 cup unsalted butter, softened
- 1 cup coconut milk (or regular milk if preferred)
- 2 large eggs
- 1 teaspoon vanilla extract
- 1/2 cup chopped walnuts or pecans (optional, for added texture)
- 1/4 cup coconut flakes (optional, for topping)

Instructions:

1. **Preheat Oven:**
   - Preheat your oven to 350°F (175°C). Grease a loaf pan or line it with parchment paper.
2. **Mix Dry Ingredients:**
   - In a large bowl, whisk together flour, shredded coconut, sugar, baking powder, and salt.
3. **Cream Butter and Sugar:**
   - In a separate bowl, cream the softened butter until smooth. Add sugar and continue to cream until light and fluffy.
4. **Combine Wet Ingredients:**
   - Beat in the eggs one at a time. Stir in coconut milk and vanilla extract until well combined.
5. **Combine Ingredients:**
   - Gradually add the dry ingredients to the wet mixture, mixing until just combined. Fold in chopped nuts if using.
6. **Pour and Smooth:**
   - Pour the batter into the prepared loaf pan and smooth the top. Sprinkle coconut flakes on top if desired.
7. **Bake:**
   - Bake for 50-60 minutes, or until the loaf is golden brown and a toothpick inserted into the center comes out clean.
8. **Cool:**
   - Allow the coconut loaf to cool in the pan for about 10 minutes before transferring to a wire rack to cool completely.

Enjoy your Martinique Coconut Loaf! It's a wonderfully tropical bread that pairs well with a cup of tea or coffee.

Curacao Pan Pita

Ingredients:

- 2 1/2 cups all-purpose flour
- 1 tablespoon sugar
- 1 tablespoon baking powder
- 1/2 teaspoon salt
- 1/4 cup vegetable oil or melted butter
- 1 cup warm water (about 110°F/45°C)
- 1 teaspoon active dry yeast (optional, for extra fluffiness)

Instructions:

1. **Prepare Yeast (Optional):**
    - If using yeast, dissolve it in 1/4 cup of the warm water with a pinch of sugar. Let it sit for 5-10 minutes until frothy.
2. **Mix Dry Ingredients:**
    - In a large bowl, whisk together flour, sugar, baking powder, and salt.
3. **Add Wet Ingredients:**
    - Create a well in the center of the dry ingredients and pour in the oil or melted butter. If using yeast, add it to the remaining warm water and pour that in as well. Mix until the dough starts to come together.
4. **Knead Dough:**
    - Turn the dough out onto a floured surface and knead for about 5-7 minutes, until smooth and elastic.
5. **Rest Dough:**
    - Cover the dough with a damp cloth and let it rest for about 30 minutes to 1 hour, or until slightly puffed.
6. **Divide and Roll:**
    - Punch down the dough and divide it into 8-10 equal pieces. Roll each piece into a flat, round shape about 1/4-inch thick.
7. **Cook:**
    - Heat a dry skillet or griddle over medium-high heat. Cook each flatbread for 1-2 minutes on each side, or until golden brown spots appear and the bread puffs slightly.
8. **Cool:**
    - Transfer the cooked Pan Pita to a wire rack to cool slightly before serving.

Enjoy your Curacao Pan Pita! It's perfect for dipping into soups or as a wrap for your favorite fillings.

Tortola Fruitcake Bread

Ingredients:

- 1 1/2 cups all-purpose flour
- 1 cup mixed dried fruit (such as raisins, currants, chopped dried apricots, or dates)
- 1/2 cup chopped nuts (such as walnuts or pecans)
- 1/2 cup brown sugar
- 1 teaspoon baking powder
- 1/2 teaspoon baking soda
- 1/2 teaspoon ground cinnamon
- 1/4 teaspoon ground nutmeg
- 1/4 teaspoon ground cloves
- 1/4 teaspoon salt
- 1/2 cup unsalted butter, softened
- 1/2 cup orange juice
- 2 large eggs
- 1 teaspoon vanilla extract
- 1/4 cup dark rum (optional, for a richer flavor)

Instructions:

1. **Preheat Oven:**
   - Preheat your oven to 350°F (175°C). Grease a loaf pan or line it with parchment paper.
2. **Mix Dry Ingredients:**
   - In a large bowl, whisk together flour, baking powder, baking soda, cinnamon, nutmeg, cloves, and salt. Stir in mixed dried fruit and chopped nuts.
3. **Cream Butter and Sugar:**
   - In a separate bowl, cream the softened butter until smooth. Add brown sugar and continue to cream until light and fluffy.
4. **Combine Wet Ingredients:**
   - Beat in the eggs one at a time. Stir in orange juice, vanilla extract, and dark rum if using.
5. **Combine Ingredients:**
   - Gradually add the dry ingredients to the wet mixture, mixing until just combined. Do not overmix.
6. **Pour and Smooth:**
   - Pour the batter into the prepared loaf pan and smooth the top.
7. **Bake:**
   - Bake for 50-60 minutes, or until the bread is golden brown and a toothpick inserted into the center comes out clean.
8. **Cool:**

- Allow the fruitcake bread to cool in the pan for about 10 minutes before transferring to a wire rack to cool completely.

Enjoy your Tortola Fruitcake Bread! It's perfect for the holidays or as a special treat throughout the year.

Saint Barthelemy Coconut Bread

Ingredients:

- 2 1/2 cups all-purpose flour
- 1 cup shredded coconut (sweetened or unsweetened, depending on your preference)
- 1/2 cup sugar
- 1 tablespoon baking powder
- 1/2 teaspoon salt
- 1/2 cup unsalted butter, softened
- 1 cup coconut milk (or regular milk if preferred)
- 2 large eggs
- 1 teaspoon vanilla extract
- 1/4 cup chopped walnuts or pecans (optional, for added texture)

Instructions:

1. **Preheat Oven:**
   - Preheat your oven to 350°F (175°C). Grease a loaf pan or line it with parchment paper.
2. **Mix Dry Ingredients:**
   - In a large bowl, whisk together flour, sugar, baking powder, salt, and shredded coconut.
3. **Cream Butter and Sugar:**
   - In a separate bowl, cream the softened butter until smooth. Add sugar and continue to cream until light and fluffy.
4. **Combine Wet Ingredients:**
   - Beat in the eggs one at a time, then stir in coconut milk and vanilla extract.
5. **Combine Ingredients:**
   - Gradually add the dry ingredients to the wet mixture, mixing until just combined. Fold in chopped nuts if using.
6. **Pour and Smooth:**
   - Pour the batter into the prepared loaf pan and smooth the top.
7. **Bake:**
   - Bake for 50-60 minutes, or until the bread is golden brown and a toothpick inserted into the center comes out clean.
8. **Cool:**
   - Allow the coconut bread to cool in the pan for about 10 minutes before transferring to a wire rack to cool completely.

Enjoy your Saint Barthélemy Coconut Bread! It's perfect for a tropical twist on your bread routine, and it pairs beautifully with a cup of coffee or tea.

Nevisian Ginger Bread

Ingredients:

- 2 1/2 cups all-purpose flour
- 1/2 cup brown sugar
- 1/4 cup molasses
- 1 tablespoon ground ginger
- 1 teaspoon ground cinnamon
- 1/2 teaspoon ground cloves
- 1/2 teaspoon baking powder
- 1/2 teaspoon baking soda
- 1/4 teaspoon salt
- 1/2 cup unsalted butter, softened
- 1 large egg
- 1 cup buttermilk (or regular milk with 1 tablespoon lemon juice or vinegar)
- 1/2 cup chopped crystallized ginger (optional, for added texture and flavor)

Instructions:

1. **Preheat Oven:**
   - Preheat your oven to 350°F (175°C). Grease a loaf pan or line it with parchment paper.
2. **Mix Dry Ingredients:**
   - In a large bowl, whisk together flour, brown sugar, ginger, cinnamon, cloves, baking powder, baking soda, and salt.
3. **Cream Butter and Sugar:**
   - In a separate bowl, cream the softened butter until smooth. Add brown sugar and continue to cream until light and fluffy.
4. **Combine Wet Ingredients:**
   - Beat in the egg, then stir in molasses and buttermilk until well combined.
5. **Combine Ingredients:**
   - Gradually add the dry ingredients to the wet mixture, mixing until just combined. Fold in chopped crystallized ginger if using.
6. **Pour and Smooth:**
   - Pour the batter into the prepared loaf pan and smooth the top.
7. **Bake:**
   - Bake for 50-60 minutes, or until the bread is golden brown and a toothpick inserted into the center comes out clean.
8. **Cool:**
   - Allow the ginger bread to cool in the pan for about 10 minutes before transferring to a wire rack to cool completely.

Enjoy your Nevisian Ginger Bread! It's a flavorful treat with a perfect blend of spices.

Anguilla Pineapple Bread

Ingredients:

- 2 1/2 cups all-purpose flour
- 1/2 cup sugar
- 1 tablespoon baking powder
- 1/2 teaspoon salt
- 1/2 teaspoon ground cinnamon (optional)
- 1/2 cup unsalted butter, softened
- 1 cup crushed pineapple, well-drained
- 1/2 cup pineapple juice (from the can or fresh)
- 2 large eggs
- 1 teaspoon vanilla extract
- 1/2 cup chopped nuts (optional, such as walnuts or pecans)
- 1/4 cup shredded coconut (optional, for extra flavor and texture)

Instructions:

1. **Preheat Oven:**
   - Preheat your oven to 350°F (175°C). Grease a loaf pan or line it with parchment paper.
2. **Mix Dry Ingredients:**
   - In a large bowl, whisk together flour, sugar, baking powder, salt, and cinnamon (if using).
3. **Cream Butter and Sugar:**
   - In a separate bowl, cream the softened butter until smooth. Add sugar and continue to cream until light and fluffy.
4. **Combine Wet Ingredients:**
   - Beat in the eggs one at a time. Stir in crushed pineapple, pineapple juice, and vanilla extract until well combined.
5. **Combine Ingredients:**
   - Gradually add the dry ingredients to the wet mixture, mixing until just combined. Fold in chopped nuts and shredded coconut if using.
6. **Pour and Smooth:**
   - Pour the batter into the prepared loaf pan and smooth the top.
7. **Bake:**
   - Bake for 50-60 minutes, or until the bread is golden brown and a toothpick inserted into the center comes out clean.
8. **Cool:**
   - Allow the pineapple bread to cool in the pan for about 10 minutes before transferring to a wire rack to cool completely.

Enjoy your Anguilla Pineapple Bread! This tropical bread is perfect as a sweet treat for breakfast or as a snack.

Saint Thomas Sweet Loaf

Ingredients:

- 3 cups all-purpose flour
- 1/2 cup sugar
- 1 tablespoon baking powder
- 1/2 teaspoon salt
- 1/2 cup unsalted butter, softened
- 1 cup milk
- 2 large eggs
- 1 teaspoon vanilla extract
- 1/2 teaspoon almond extract (optional, for added flavor)
- 1/4 cup chopped nuts or dried fruit (optional, for texture)

Instructions:

1. **Preheat Oven:**
   - Preheat your oven to 350°F (175°C). Grease a loaf pan or line it with parchment paper.
2. **Mix Dry Ingredients:**
   - In a large bowl, whisk together flour, sugar, baking powder, and salt.
3. **Cream Butter and Sugar:**
   - In a separate bowl, cream the softened butter until smooth. Add sugar and continue to cream until light and fluffy.
4. **Combine Wet Ingredients:**
   - Beat in the eggs one at a time, then stir in milk, vanilla extract, and almond extract if using.
5. **Combine Ingredients:**
   - Gradually add the dry ingredients to the wet mixture, mixing until just combined. Fold in chopped nuts or dried fruit if desired.
6. **Pour and Smooth:**
   - Pour the batter into the prepared loaf pan and smooth the top.
7. **Bake:**
   - Bake for 50-60 minutes, or until the loaf is golden brown and a toothpick inserted into the center comes out clean.
8. **Cool:**
   - Allow the sweet loaf to cool in the pan for about 10 minutes before transferring to a wire rack to cool completely.

Enjoy your Saint Thomas Sweet Loaf! It's a delicious treat for breakfast or a light snack.

www.ingramcontent.com/pod-product-compliance
Lightning Source LLC
LaVergne TN
LVHW081617060526
838201LV00054B/2284